# Social Behavior and Self-Management

## 5-Point Scales for Adolescents and Adults

Kari Dunn Buron, MS
Jane Thierfeld Brown, EdD
Mitzi Curtis, MA
Lisa King, MEd

*Foreword by Stephen Shore, EdD*

**PUBLISHING**
P.O. Box 23173
Shawnee Mission, Kansas 66283-0173
www.aapcpublishing.net

# AAPC
**PUBLISHING**

©2012 AAPC Publishing
P.O. Box 23173
Shawnee Mission, Kansas 66283-0173
www.aapcpublishing.net

Publisher's Cataloging-in-Publication

Social behavior and self-management : 5-point scales for adolescents and adults / Kari Dunn Buron ... [et al.] ; foreword by Stephen Shore. -- Shawnee Mission, Kan. : AAPC Publishing, c2012.

p. ; cm.

ISBN: 978-1-934575-91-8
LCCN: 2012943710
Includes bibliographical references.
Summary: Practical tools and other resources to help adolescents and adults improve their social success through better self-regulation, improved interpretation of social cues and other interpersonal skills, in order to lead successful independent lives.

1. Autistic youth--Behavior modification. 2. Autistic people--Behavior modification. 3. Autism spectrum disorders--Patients--Behavior modification. 4. Autistic youth--Life skills guides.
5. Autism spectrum disorders--Patients--Life skills guides. 6. Social skills in adolescence--Study and teaching. 7. Social skills--Study and teaching. 8. Social interaction in adolescence--Study and teaching. 9. Social interaction--Study and teaching.
10. Interpersonal relations in adolescence--Study and teaching.
11. Interpersonal relations--Study and teaching. I. Buron, Kari Dunn. II. Title.

RC553.A88 S63 2012
616.85882--dc23                                              1209

This book is designed in Helvetica Neue and Century Schoolbook.

Printed in the United States of America.

# Acknowledgments

Our thanks go to Lorraine Wolf, Christine Wenzel, Megan Krell and Michelle Rigler.

A special thanks also goes to the Autism Society of Minnesota and the following adults, who took the time to meet with us and selflessly give us their advice:

Donald Sweet
Claire Sisson
Larry Moody
Pete Jarnstrom
Matthew Harvie
Rich Settergren
Paul Johnson
TJ Neumiller
Lisa Sanders
Dianna Chabot
Bryan Carlson
Catlin Payton

*We dedicate this book to our wonderful friend,
colleague and co-author, Lisa King,
in support of her fight against
the beast that is breast cancer.*

# Table of Contents

# Foreword

**B**oy, do I wish I had something like this when I was in my adolescent through younger adult years, as I worked my way through college and into my first "real" jobs. Although I did not externalize meltdowns, there are a number of times when I could have used the help provided in this latest of the growing series of 5-Point Scale books for managing my social behavior and my emotions, thereby bringing about greater understanding of my feelings and more successful interactions with others.

This resource fills a yawning gap in the toolbox of interventions that typically have been so heavily weighted towards children on the autism spectrum. Eventually, those children grow up to become adults on the autism spectrum, suggesting an imperative to develop interventions, methods, and techniques for supporting the ever-increasing population of people with autism transitioning through adolescence and into adulthood.

Traditionally, efforts to address the challenges people with autism and related conditions have in understanding the social and emotional aspects of life have focused on shoring up weaknesses. In contrast, this book joins others in a new paradigm of employing the strengths of people on the autism spectrum to help them become more fluent in this important aspect of life. Logic and ranking of data or information are strengths for many on the autism spectrum. The authors take advantage of this characteristic to systemize and bring order by rating the most vexing parts of social interaction and emotional regulation in ways people on the autism spectrum and related conditions can easily process and understand.

Rather than subscribing to the myth that individuals on the autism spectrum have no or stunted emotional lives, the authors expertly address the twin challenges of understanding, verbalizing, and ranking emotions as well as the social impact of our actions. For example, ranking positive emotions from calmness to hope to pleasure, to joy and, finally, elation, helps individuals on the autism spectrum understand the "grey" areas between the two extremes. The gradations of sadness – from having no issues at all or being "a little down" to complete devastation – are addressed in the same way. Other scales related to being overwhelmed or relaxed round out the variety of emotions individuals with autism – as well as everyone else – experience in their day-to-day lives.

Another area of challenge for individuals with autism pertains to understanding the effects of one's behavior on others. There is a myth that people with autism don't wish to socialize. In reality, what seems to happen is that, due to a lack of awareness of how one's behaviors are interpreted by others, attempts to interact often go badly. Repetition of this outcome causes the person to give up trying.

For example, suppose an individual with autism is interested in dating somebody, and fails to understand that after three unsuccessful attempts to arrange a meeting, it's time to stop. Indeed, continuing to pursue the other individual could lead to stalking behavior resulting in possible involvement with the police. However, by using a 5-Point Scale as a way to interpret how others might perceive one's behavior, as is done with the *Stalking Scale,* the individual on the autism spectrum has a way of gauging how his or her actions affect others. A potentially traumatic encounter with law enforcement is now avoided in favor of a milder disappointment upon realizing that dating efforts should be focused elsewhere.

In a similar manner, the 5-Point Scale can be used to rank and differentiate between different levels of relationships – ranging from stranger and acquaintance to intimate relationship or spouse. By defining these relationships, the individual with autism can more accurately gauge and manage both behavior and emotions.

Finally, in keeping with the adage of "teaching a man to fish" as a means of lifelong education rather than giving him a fish that will satisfy him for but one day, readers are encouraged to use what they learn from this book to develop their own 5-Point Scales in the moment as situations crop up. I know I will be doing that, and I will recommend the same to my friends on the autism spectrum.

Once again, AAPC Publishing is at the forefront – this time by providing time-tested, practical solutions for the ever-increasing numbers of adults with autism and related conditions. By capitalizing on the way individuals with autism process information and learn, this latest volume in the 5-Point Scale series brings comprehending emotions, their gradations, and managing social behavior to new heights. For those supporting individuals on the autism spectrum, as well as those with autism, this book represents an invaluable tool for making lives better for adults with autism and related conditions.

Stephen M. Shore, EdD

Assistant professor of special education, internationally renowned author, consultant, and presenter on issues related to autism; person on the autism spectrum

# Preface

By Kari Dunn Buron and Mitzi Curtis

**N**atural social order, such as who is in charge and who is supposed to follow, is not always obvious to the person with ASD (autism spectrum disorder). The world may appear chaotic, and the social rules of everyday interaction can seem confusing, unreasonable and unfair. A person on the autism spectrum may not understand nonverbal social language such as facial expressions and, therefore, miss the social cues needed to size up a social situation. Such social confusion can lead to stress and anxiety, and even offensive behavior.

We have learned that individuals with ASD tend to understand social information better when it is explained to them using visual systems. For example, Simon Baron-Cohen (2009) suggests that if individuals with ASD possess effective systematizing skills (the ability to figure out systems), they may be able to use those skills to compensate for difficulties in empathizing skills (ability to understand social and emotional concepts). An example of this would be to use a flow chart to logically work through various behaviors and the emotions they provoke. Tony Attwood (2006) lends support to this idea, stating that the more someone with ASD understands about his or her emotions, the more able that person is to express them appropriately.

*The Incredible 5-Point Scale* (Buron & Curtis, 2012) introduced the use of a scale as a way of explaining social and emotional concepts to individuals who have difficulty understanding such information but have a relative strength in understanding systems. Let's look at an example. A person who offends others with blunt or offensive remarks may learn to understand the negative effects of his behavior through the use of a scale.

Using the following scale, a support person can outline how that person's behavior influences the way others think about him and list some natural outcomes. Using the scale in this way seems to make such discussions less personal and easier to engage in without defensiveness. The key here is for the support person to be *concrete and nonjudgmental* in the use of words. It is not a character flaw you are dealing with but a lack of skills, not unlike a social learning disability.

| Rating | What You Said | How the Other Person Might Feel | What This Might Mean |
|---|---|---|---|
| **5** | I could kill you! You would be better off dead! | Afraid Threatened | They might call the police or campus security. This is very serious and could get you arrested! |
| **4** | Swearing This assignment is ridiculous! | Nervous Possibly threatened | The person might not want to be around you. An instructor might not want you in her class. A boss might fire you. |
| **3** | Telling someone he is fat or stupid | Offended Sad | The person might think you are unkind and uncaring and may not want to be around you or work with you. |
| **2** | Talking to someone during class while the instructor is talking | Confused Worried Uncomfortable | The instructor might have unfriendly thoughts about you when the time comes to assign grades and, therefore, give you a lower grade. The person you are talking to might not want to sit near you. |
| **1** | Smiling at someone at work. Talking with someone at break time using kind words | Comfortable Relaxed | You might keep more friends. This can help you get along at work. |

Use of the 5-Point Scale has not only been helpful for supporting school-aged students but has more recently been found to be successful with adults who continue to struggle with social and emotional information.

When adults on the autism spectrum leave the protective environment of their home or the familiar structure of school, it can be difficult for them to find ways to effectively address their support needs. The 5-Point Scale can be used to increase communication between the person on the spectrum and her support person. It can also increase self-management skills and, once learned, can serve as a self-advocacy tool. For example, if a person unexpectedly finds herself in a confusing social dilemma, the scale can be used as a consistent format for the caregiver or support person to process the problem.

*Scales should be co-created with the person whenever possible.* They should clearly describe the behavior and strategies and types of support that he or she might need. Remember, as a caregiver, you are not "telling" the person what to do; you are jointly working out the problem and developing solutions that can increase competence and independence.

Co-creating scales increases social understanding for both parties. It sends a clear message that the support person is agreeing to take into consideration the difficulties the person with ASD may encounter and to provide reasonable accommodations to minimize discomfort and social misunderstanding. The person with ASD, in turn, receives information regarding the perspectives and actions of other people in his environment, as well as how his behavior impacts others – be it on the job, at college, on a date, or at a family gathering.

The scales can also give direction to others, such as bosses, social workers, family members and/or partners, who are interacting with the person with ASD. For example, a scale might indicate that when the person on the spectrum is highly anxious, continued talking on the part of the support person will likely increase the stress. This helps the boss or family member know how to monitor their own behavior during difficult interactions. The scale supports everyone involved and can lead to agreements about what to do, and what not to do, in a given situation.

# Introduction

This book was developed as a support tool for anyone advocating for, living with or working with an adult on the autism spectrum. *The Incredible 5-Point Scale* (Buron & Curtis, 2012) introduced this simple, yet very effective tool but gave only school-aged examples of how to use the scale. The current book includes examples of scales used to support individuals to better understand 15 different social situations. The ideas presented in these examples reflect actual situations reported by adult service providers, as well as interviews with more than 20 adults on the autism spectrum.

In Part One, common issues are discussed. These are issues that the authors have encountered while working with or interviewing adults on the spectrum. For each issue or problem, we ...

- Offer information to caregiver and support networks regarding the selected social issues and how they might affect someone's social performance. This explanation can be useful for those in legal departments, job coaches/bosses, families and teachers by helping them to understand the nature of social cognition and emotional regulation and how these issues can impact social behavior.

- Provide an example of scales that may be used to address the specific issue. **It is important to remember that the scales illustrated are examples only. They are not meant to be used verbatim.**

- Provide an example of how a caregiver or support person might explain the social situation or concept to the person on the spectrum. These suggestions use very concrete, black-and-white language, while attempting to avoid judgmental statements. They are not meant to be scripts but to serve as a guide or springboard for a more individualized discussion.

The first three topics and scales are all related to emotional regulation and control of emotions in difficult situations. Emotional regulation is so often at the root of troublesome behaviors or a person's inability to cope with day-to-day expectations that we felt it warranted being discussed from three different angles – emotional regulation, feeling overwhelmed and relaxation.

The remaining topics and scales are designed to teach social concepts that, if not mastered, can significantly disrupt a person's ability to accurately define, understand and negotiate social situations and expectations.

Part Two presents concrete examples of how, once the idea of the scale is understood, the strategy may be used to address troubling issues as they arise.

With these examples as your guide, we are hoping you will ...

- Understand the nature of ASD, and social cognition in particular
- Recognize the impact social anxiety has on behavior and judgment
- Be able to systematically process social difficulties to increase clarity from a variety of perspectives
- Be able to clearly outline specific ideas for handling future situations.

# Part One:
# Using Scales With Young Adults

In this section, we will give specific examples of how you can make use of the 5-Point Scale to support your family member, student, employee or client. The examples we have chosen involve a broad range of social topics that can present problems for young adults on the autism spectrum. These examples are not exhaustive, but are intended to provide the foundation you need to begin creating similar scales specific to your own unique situation and concerns.

As well as defining the nine topic areas and illustrating one or more scales for each topic, we offer suggestions for discussing the issue with the person you support. Autism involves difficulty with social and emotional language concepts, and it is often helpful to discuss such topics using very direct, concrete, yet compassionate language.

# Topic: Emotional Regulation

People on the autism spectrum tend to have difficulty understanding and defining emotions in themselves as well as recognizing various emotions in others. This interpersonal life skill is often referred to as "emotional regulation," or the ability to accurately assess the presenting situation and respond in a reasonable way.

Do you ever find that your adult child, student or employee seems to "overreact" or "under-react" to situations? Just asking him to "settle down" or "stop being so sensitive" is likely to confuse and frustrate a person who is feeling emotion intensely at the moment, and that is likely to decrease his ability to think clearly. If this happens often, it is a good idea to assume that the person may have a problem with emotional regulation.

Emotional regulation can also involve under-responding to emotional situations. For example, some life event may occur that everyone in the family or everyone at work finds devastating (loss of life or an accident of some kind). Family members and coworkers are expecting an emotional response but might get no response, or little emotion, from the person with ASD.

*The 5-Point Scale is a way of studying emotions in a very structured and logical way.* Through the use of a scale, you can help the person "think through" various situations at a time when she is calm and in control. If the person can agree that a bad grade is upsetting, for example, but not as horrible as flunking out of school, then you can establish a starting point for discussing helpful ways of dealing with the emotion that emerges when she gets a bad grade.

It is helpful to talk about how that emotion makes her body feel so that she can recognize it when it starts. Another idea is to talk about how she thinks about the situation. If she reports that when she gets a bad grade she thinks it is "horrible," then logically pointing out that it is more like "unfortunate" might help her to rethink her thinking.

Using analogies can also be helpful. For example, on her road to academic success, a bad grade might be a pothole (unfortunate and even bothersome, but it does not prevent her from going forward). You can compare the pothole to a closed road (this might be a failing grade) or the need to find a new map (change in major area of study).

Another example of working through emotional regulation is handling rejection from a peer. Perhaps the person with ASD was attracted to somebody and asked that person out on a date but was turned down. This would be hard on anyone, but realistically it is probably a "3" (upsetting, but not devastating). For the person with ASD, it might very well feel devastating, and thus evoke a very big emotion. Working through scenarios like this can be helpful in preparing the person for the everyday ups and downs of adult life.

The following are two examples of how a scale might be used to teach the various degrees of interpersonal emotional reactions. These are followed by check-in scales. Again, it is important to remember that these are only examples. Each scale should be developed so that it reflects the issues specific to the person you are working with.

## Defining Interpersonal Emotions

| 5 | **Love.** This is the strongest emotion. You might feel like you want to be with this person all of the time. This emotion usually involves physical desire. This emotion takes time to nurture and grow. This might include sexual love but doesn't have to. |
|---|---|
| 4 | **Sexually attracted to someone.** This is a very strong feeling of being physically attracted to someone. Wanting to be with this person a lot. This might or might not include caring for the person in other ways. This can be confused with love. |
| 3 | **Caring for someone.** At this level, you want to be with this person and share activities; maybe go to a movie or sporting event. This might include physical attraction but not always. |
| 2 | **Liking someone.** This level involves noticing the other person and being interested in talking to the person or getting along with the person. |
| 1 | **No attraction at all.** At this level, there is no interest, thought or feeling about the other person as being different from anybody else. |

*Note.* One way to use this scale might be to have the person rate how he feels about certain people he knows and how he thinks others might feel about him.

## Studying Basic POSITIVE Emotions

| Rating | Feelings | What Could Make You Feel This Way? |
|---|---|---|
| **5** | Elation<br>Ecstatic<br>Enthralled<br>Excited | Being with someone you love and trust; having an opportunity to do something great; starting a new adventure.<br><br>You? |
| **4** | Joy<br>Cheerfulness<br>Zest<br>Optimism | A compliment; finishing a project; competing in an activity you are good at.<br><br>You? |
| **3** | Pleasure<br>Pride<br>Happy | Getting a good grade; winning a game; creating something.<br><br>You? |
| **2** | Hope<br>Satisfaction<br>Serene | Being with friends; talking with a parent; petting a dog.<br><br>You? |
| **1** | Calm<br>Content<br>Relaxed | Being alone; thinking about your favorite things; sleeping.<br><br>You? |

*Note.* Now try it for basic negative emotions.

## *Check-in Scales*

If you are working with or supporting someone who is unable to control explosive behavior, it is a good idea to break down the person's ability to control various situations by creating a 5-Point Scale. Each level should describe situations that make the person feel good, OK, upset, angry and explosive. Once the different levels are established, the person can then begin to proactively assess his tolerance levels and keep track of early signs of stress. That is, with support, the person can determine which situations might be too overwhelming for him and where he might need some help.

The "check-in" scale provides a predictable and systematic way of assessing various levels of stress even when the person is calm. An important first step in controlling one's emotions is to recognize early signs of nervousness and anxiety. If a person can identify these feelings by checking in daily, or even several times a day, he is better able address the stressful feelings in a positive way.

Because each situation is different, a plan has to be individualized for the person you are working with. In the beginning, the check-in idea might seem rather energy and time intensive, but as the person learns the system, he should be able to do body check-ins on his own.

People can learn to keep track of their emotions and their successes by recording their check-in sessions, whether monitored by a support person or not. Monitoring their check-ins might take the form of a chart or journal; an example of success might be rating oneself at a 3 (upset or nervous) and, as a result, choosing to take a quiet walk at break time or between classes to avoid further escalation.

The following is an example of a blank check-in scale.

## Check-in Scale

| Rating | What This Looks Like | What This Feels Like | I Can Try to Do This | The Support I Can Get |
|--------|----------------------|----------------------|----------------------|-----------------------|
| 5 | | | | |
| 4 | | | | |
| 3 | | | | |
| 2 | | | | |
| 1 | | | | |

# *Ideas and Words to Use When Explaining Issues of Emotional Control to a Person With ASD*

- Emotional regulation refers to how your brain and body work together to handle strong feelings. This can involve both negative and positive emotions. Either way, it is almost always hard to think clearly when you are faced with **big emotions.**

- When a big emotion hits (love, hate, anger, remorse, etc.), your brain becomes "compromised" by that feeling. If you are not prepared, the emotional responses take over and make it hard for your brain to think about the best way to respond. You might say hurtful things to someone that you don't really mean; you might feel like you are having a panic attack; or you might even feel like lashing out physically. All of these responses are likely to happen at some time in your life, but if they happen too often, it becomes a problem.
- One way to begin to think about how to handle big emotions is to think clearly about the different levels of emotion. Some emotions are really big for everybody, like love or hatred. Other emotions can be thought of as small, such as irritation. When you think about an emotion as being big or small, it can make it easier to break down and identify each part of the emotion and label how it might feel and how you might logically respond to it. You can do this with a numerical scale. For example, think about the emotion "sad." Now think about the following scale applied to "sad" and the varying degrees of being sad.

**5 = Devastated/heartbroken/depressed** – This is intense sadness. A person will usually need some help to work through this level of sadness.
**4 = Very sad** – Something personal happened that might make you cry and feel like you can hardly talk about it.
**3 = Upset/feel like crying** – A sad movie can make you feel like this. You feel the emotion, but it is not really directly related to your life.
**2 = A little down** – Maybe you are disappointed about something, such as the grocery store being out of your preferred brand of milk.
**1 = No issues** – But maybe you are feeling a bit melancholy.

Using this general scale, you can think about something that might happen to make you feel sad at each of the levels. If someone you know and love dies, it is likely you will feel like a 5. You probably need some help from a support person before you will feel better. The people you are close to will understand that you are intensely sad, and they will usually want to help. If you get a poor grade on an assignment, it is probably more worthy of a 2 feeling. The people around you will likely think that your emotion about a poor grade will be about 2, or maybe 3. If you become devastated (a 5) about a bad grade, it will be surprising to the people around you, and they won't be as likely to think that you need support.

In the previous scale, you might think that going to the grocery store and finding that they are out of your favorite food should be a 4 or a 5. This is OK, but that would be what many people would consider an "over-reaction," or too much emotion for the situation. Rating various situations is a great place to start working on understanding emotions.

# Topic: Feeling Overwhelmed

Individuals on the autism spectrum easily become overwhelmed by day-to-day tasks, social interactions and events. For example, we interviewed a group of adults and asked them to list some potential problems.

Here are some of their responses: last-minute changes, being asked to do too many things at one time, having to prioritize chores or jobs, paying bills and handling social encounters.

Many of these adults mentioned that they had developed coping strategies to soothe their anxiety, such as going to a quiet place to think or taking a walk. Some reported that they had used less healthy methods, such as drinking alcohol, taking street drugs, or resorting to excessive social isolation.

Many individuals with ASD have difficulty seeing the "gray areas" of social relationships and, therefore, misread situations time and time again. Such rigid thinking tends to lead people to judge themselves and others rather harshly when things don't go as planned.

Somebody might be able to deal with one or even two irritating events, but when a third thing happens, she might respond in an aggressive way. To support folks, this "third thing" might look very minor, like a late bus, and, therefore, be assessed as unreasonable behavior. In reality, the issue is more of an ongoing accumulation of frustrations and, therefore, the solution must reflect that.

Some adults with ASD report that support people in their lives, no matter how well meaning, actually add to the problem by "nagging" them or giving them too much advice. A scale can be used to rate one's need for support given specific situations.

The following is an example of a scale used by a person who was easily overwhelmed. It is not meant to be used as is but to serve as a guide for developing coping scales for individuals with similar issues.

## Ongoing Rating to Keep From Feeling Overwhelmed

| Rating | Tell Me Something Good | Things Gone Wrong | What Do I Need? |
|--------|-----------------------|-------------------|-----------------|
| 5 | | | I think I need a total break from work or school. |
| 4 | | | I think I need some serious support. |
| 3 | | | I could use some chat time right now. |
| 2 | | | Maybe I should check in an extra time this week. |
| 1 | | | No particular needs |

*Note.* In this example, the person sat down with his support person at various scheduled times throughout the week. They talked about and listed good stuff from the top down. Then they listed things that had gone wrong, from the bottom up. This gave a visual picture of the balance of good and bad.

## Another Example of a Scale to Monitor the Need for Support

| Rating | I Feel: | You Will Be Able to Tell Because: | This Is the Level of Support I Need: |
|---|---|---|---|
| **5** | I feel the worst I have ever felt. | I will leave. I might go without saying a word. I will avoid people. | I really want you to know I'm upset, but please do not talk to me. |
| **4** | I'm feeling pretty bad right now. | I might just go to sleep. My hair and clothes might be dirty. | Write me a note to ask what is wrong. Give me some time. |
| **3** | I'm feeling OK right now, but a little down. | I'll stick around, but I'm quiet. I might be unshaved. | Ask me if I want to talk. Keep tabs on me but don't crowd me. |
| **2** | I'm feeling pretty relaxed right now. | I can go to work or class. | No extra help needed. Maybe check in from time to time. |
| **1** | Right now I'm great! | Happy; will talk a lot and share. | Nothing extra. I am just fine. |

## *Ideas and Words to Use When Explaining Issues of Feeling Overwhelmed to a Person With ASD*

- Feeling overwhelmed is not a good feeling. It might feel like the world is out to get you or that nothing ever goes your way. You might have racing thoughts with no sign of a solution. If you often feel like you are losing control of your life, it is important to ask for help.
- Some adults have reported that taking a long walk along a familiar route is a great way to calm the nerves and give the brain time to work out confusing and negative thoughts. Taking a walk when you first start feeling overwhelmed is often a good idea and can keep you

from losing control of your words. When someone feels that their life is out of control, they are likely to panic, and panic can lead to things like swearing at your boss or threatening someone.

- Although walking away from a problem can be the right thing to do "in the moment," it is important to sit down and work out some ideas to help you stay in control. Some things that might help are visual schedules or task lists to keep in your pocket and help you stay on track. Another good idea is to try checking in with a support person on a scheduled basis so you can process your worries and frustrations as they come up rather than letting them build.

- Using a 5-Point Scale can help you quickly let your support person know "where you are" on the overwhelmed scale. Do you just need a little direction or are you feeling depressed and unable to function? Depression can be a very serious issue, and you should have someone to talk to about it. The scale makes it easier to map out a plan that both you and your support person can agree on.

# Topic: Relaxation

As a family member or support person for a person with ASD, it is important to understand that ASD is first and foremost a social disorder. Given this, social situations of any kind (roommates, interaction with teachers, taking direction from a supervisor, etc.) can cause stress and anxiety. These are likely to be lifelong issues for someone with ASD and, therefore, it makes sense to spend some time helping the person learn more about relaxation in general.

Simply asking a person with ASD to "calm down" is not an effective approach. It is best to help an anxious person to find a preferred method of relaxation, something he can participate in on a regular basis.

Yoga, the martial arts, tai chi, meditation, swimming and walking are all examples of activities that can benefit a person with social anxieties. By engaging in this type of activity on a regular basis (daily or every other day), the person is more likely to be in tune with his bodily reactions to stress, and more able to recognize and control negative responses. Most university settings and many apartment complexes offer access to swimming pools and/or exercise facilities. If the person you support does not have immediate access to such facilities, the YMCA/YWCA program, community centers and commercial fitness centers offer opportunities in these areas. Walking as a routine part of one's day is an excellent form of relaxation. Most indoor malls and some large sporting facilities have walking programs free to the public when climate conditions make walking out-of-doors difficult.

Other forms of relaxation include such things as reading, puzzling, knitting and doing needlepoint. An adult with ASD reported that thinking about his special interest helped to keep him calm. He scheduled times throughout the day when he could close his eyes and think about baseball statistics. This helped him to remain calm during other parts of his day.

When using the 5-Point Scale, help the person to identify situations that typically cause the most stress, as well as situations that don't bother her at all. This can help her understand that there are predictably stressful situations in life and that it is good to plan for them.

After you have identified stressful times, it is important to discuss how the different levels of stress might feel. Early awareness of stress is the best way to avoid unfortunate – extreme – reactions, and individual relaxation strategies are most effective if they are used early on in the stress cycle. For example, does the person get a stomachache when initially faced with frustration? If so, teaching her to close her eyes and take a few slow, deep breaths at the first sign of a stomachache can help to curb the stress. Does she feel like she is being flooded with stress throughout her whole body? Identifying how she feels when becoming stressed can help her recognize when it is time to stop what she is doing and focus on relaxing.

Another good idea is to assess how the person *thinks* about social situations. If he begins to think that the world is unfair or unjust, this could mean that his stress level is climbing from an "in-control" 2 level to a nervous or fearful 3 level. This negative thinking might be a message that his stress level is rising and that he might avoid a loss of control by stopping and using some predetermined relaxation strategies, such as affirmation cards. Affirmation cards are small cards that can fit in a pocket, backpack or purse. They contain short positive statements about the person and can be read periodically to help minimize negative thinking. For example, "I am capable," "I am smart and I can do this," or "This too shall pass."

Because social situations are, by nature, unpredictable, teaching the person with ASD how to use immediate relaxation strategies can be very helpful. Immediate actions might include closing his eyes, taking deep breaths, or rubbing his arms and legs. A short routine of these relaxing actions can be practiced along with the traditional forms of relaxation mentioned previously. The routine should be easy to do, easy to remember and possible to do in almost any situation.

Here are a few ideas to consider when teaching a short relaxation routine:
- It should be taught and practiced when the person is calm.
- It should be easy for the person to do.
- It should be practiced in real-life situations to assess its effectiveness.

Relaxation routines include:
- closing eyes to shut out stimulation
- taking slow, deep breaths to get oxygen to the brain
- engaging in positive self-talk like "I can do this" or "I am capable" to counteract any negative thinking
- squeezing hand to help calm the fight-or-flight[1] physiological symptoms
- visualizing a favorite place or a favorite thing

Teaching the person you support about relaxation can help him navigate those unexpected but inevitable stressful situations we all encounter every day. Any overt negative behavior should be carefully analyzed as it relates to stress, since a loss of control is almost always connected to big emotions.

The following two scales are examples of how you might address relaxation with the person you support. Remember that these scales are only examples. Your scale should reflect the specific issues related to the person you are supporting or working with.

---

1. The fight-or-flight response refers to a fight-or-flight-or-freeze response, hyperarousal, or acute stress response.

# Relaxation Scale

| Rating | How Does This Feel? | What Can I Do About It? |
|---|---|---|
| **5** | Horrible! I feel like I have lost control. I want to hit something or break something. | It is too late to use many of the relaxation tools. Stop talking. Close your eyes and try to slow down your breathing. Avoid looking at the person or thing you are upset with. |
| **4** | It feels like I am being flooded with bad feelings. I feel like I am going to argue with someone. | End the interaction you are engaged in (phone call, discussion, computer game, etc.). Stop talking and walk away to somewhere more isolated. |
| **3** | I have a stomachache. I know I am upset and nervous and a little fearful. | This is a perfect time to use your relaxation strategies. Leave the situation, if possible. Do deep breathing and meditation. Think of your favorite place. Continue relaxing until you feel calm. |
| **2** | I feel a little nervous. This is like a day when I will be expected to do something that is difficult for me. | Do some sort of relaxation (yoga, meditation, tai chi, etc.) before you leave your room or apartment. Be aware that it might be a difficult day and bring some affirmation cards in your wallet or backpack – read them several times during the day. |
| **1** | I feel good. I am relaxed and sure of my schedule and expectations. I am prepared for class or work. | It is always good to do your predetermined relaxation exercises before leaving home in the morning. Sometimes meditating at lunch can keep you relaxed and successful. |

## Relaxation Scale – Another Example

| Rating | How I Feel | What Should I Do? |
|---|---|---|
| **5** | Out of control! | Get help immediately from whomever has been identified as your safe person. |
| **4** | Angry or really upset. | Stop! Walk away. Go somewhere quiet like your bedroom, a bathroom or a study area. |
| **3** | Nervous. Feeling life is unfair. Ruminating over something negative. | Danger zone. Now is a good time to leave the situation, go home or take a break. Take deep breaths. Avoid talking to people or sending e-mails or texts. |
| **2** | Not great but not bad. | Stay the course. Remember to do your daily relaxation. |
| **1** | Great! I am doing one of my favorite things. Totally relaxed. | Enjoy this feeling. Make a note of how you are feeling and what things are helping you feel this way. |

# *Ideas and Words to Use When Explaining the Importance of Relaxation to a Person With ASD*

- Stress can interfere with how you think. When you are in a social situation and you are either unsure of what to do or you feel overwhelmed by the demands, stress can make it harder for you to make a good decision or respond in a positive way.
- When you feel stressed, your emotions can take over and cause you to overreact or to react impulsively. It is a good idea to learn how to relax in stressful situations. The important part about relaxation is to use relaxing strategies throughout the day so that your brain is more flexible when you face frustration.

For example, if you are working on something important and your roommate is playing loud music, you might become stressed out and angry. Your anger can then trigger a bad reaction, like yelling at your roommate. If you have practiced relaxation, you might be able to take a few deep breaths to calm yourself down and then calmly ask your roommate to turn his music down. If your brain can remain relaxed, you might also decide that going to the library or another quiet spot to study would be a good idea. *These healthy reactions are only possible if you are able to stay relaxed and in control.*

- It is a good idea to find some sort of relaxation that you enjoy and that you can do every day, like yoga poses, swimming, meditation or tai chi. This is good for both your body and your mind.
- Another good idea is to practice a routine of relaxing movements. This is something that you can do when you are faced with those unexpected moments that inevitably occur. This might look something like this:
  - Close eyes
  - Breathe in slowly and deeply and hold your breath for a few seconds
  - Slowly exhale and say to yourself, "I can handle this."

When using a 5-Point Scale to rate situations you find stressful, it is important to note that the most beneficial time to use relaxing strategies is when you are at a 1 or 2 (OK or just a little stressed). This is because those frustrating emotions can get very big, very fast, and if you aren't aware of them, they can get away from you.

Completing a scale with a support person can help you think about things like how your body feels when you begin to get irritated or nervous about a situation and how it feels when you are about to lose control. You can then use the scale to map out your plan for using relaxation. When your body feels like a 4 or a 5, you will need to use those short, quick routines mentioned previously.

# Topic: Stalking Behavior

*The following three issues can easily lead to problems in this area:*

1. Most individuals on the autism spectrum are probably interested in a social life on some level.
2. People on the autism spectrum have difficulty with nonverbal social communication. They have problems communicating effectively with their bodies, and they have difficulty "reading" another person's body language accurately.
3. Difficulty with reading others' emotions and intentions can lead to social confusion and result in poor social problem solving.

If you put these three issues together, it is easy to see how someone with ASD might be interested in having a romantic relationship but lack the skills to do it in a way that makes the other person feel comfortable.

An employer might fire a person because coworkers are not comfortable around that person. This kind of social situation is difficult to talk about, so the real reason for firing the person might be left unsaid, leaving the person with ASD confused about why he was let go. In this situation, the person with ASD never gets the feedback that might help him change his patterns of social interaction. A scale can provide the forum to give him this much-needed support.

Problems related to nonverbal social communication can cause others to distrust a person, overreact and feel threatened. This "misreading" of the person's behavior may lead to charges of "stalking" even when the person is innocent of any malicious intent.

If the person you are supporting has ever been misinterpreted in this way, it is critical to help him to recognize his social errors. A scale can help him understand the various levels of behavior and is a way to systematically suggest ideas for correcting a social error. The scale can visually show how other people might react to an unexpected social behavior.

Disclosure, or telling someone about one's disability, is sometimes necessary if the person's body language is odd but she hasn't confided that she has autism. Counseling can help the person with ASD to better understand how the issue of nonverbal social communication might lead to being misunderstood. Seeking out direct social skills training or support might also be an option for such a person.

Some young adults feel misjudged or unfairly treated when you tell them that they must modify their behavior. However, this is a very serious issue, and they might need to learn that there are certain things you just cannot do, even if you don't understand the reasons why. An example might be: You should not tell your boss to "stick it," even if you are thinking it. Another example might be: You cannot tell a co-worker that his project idea is stupid, even if you think it is.

As a support person, if you notice problems in this area, address them as directly and formally as possible. This is a time to be gentle but absolutely honest. The following stalking scales were used to help two individuals on the spectrum. Everyone's scale will be a little different depending on personality, level of social understanding and the specifics of their circumstances.

## Stalking Scale #1

| Rating | What Might This Look Like? | What Might This Make Someone Else Think? |
|---|---|---|
| 5 | Calling repetitively every day. Going to someone's house uninvited. Saying something that feels threatening to the other person. | You are too scary. You might be dangerous and I can't take a chance that you will hurt me. I need to call the police. |
| 4 | Asking someone out on a date when they have said "no" more than three times. Calling someone and talking about sexual or violent topics. Staring at someone for more than 60 seconds. | This person does not understand that I never want to go out with him. I am a little afraid because of the topics he talks about. I might need some help with this problem. |
| 3 | Singing a song to a girl in the cafeteria because you think she is pretty. Sitting down at the same table in the cafeteria but then not saying anything. | This person is hard to understand. He is odd, and that makes him unpredictable. I feel uncomfortable around him. |
| 2 | Calling someone for a date, and after three "no" answers, not calling her about a date again. Going to someone's dorm room or apartment when invited. | This is a reasonable and friendly person. I am not afraid of this person because he seems to understand social rules. |
| 1 | Not talking to other people at all. Sitting alone in the cafeteria. Working quietly in the library. | This person is not dangerous, but he's not very friendly. This person might be shy, but I am not afraid of him. |

# Stalking Scale #2 – Examples of Rethinking Your Thinking

| Rating | This Is My First Thought | This Is How I Can Rethink the Situation |
|---|---|---|
| 5 | I must have a date. I deserve a date with a pretty girl. She needs to call me back. I will call her again or go over to her house. | Stop! I cannot push the issue of dates. This is rigid, absolute thinking. If she said "no" three times, she is not going to change her mind. Going to her house will make her think I am stalking. This could be very dangerous for me. |
| 4 | I think about sexual things when I see this person. I want to share my sexual thoughts to see if she feels the same way. | Wait! Sexual thoughts are private thoughts. Although many people have sexual thoughts, they do not talk about them. I need to keep my sexual thoughts silent unless I am talking to someone I have a serious relationship with. |
| 3 | I see the girl I would like to date. I will go over to her table and sit down so that she will notice me. Maybe I will sit next to her in class and pull my chair real close to her chair. | The best way to meet someone new is to either have someone introduce me or wait until the person is naturally nearby and not busy and then introduce myself. Just putting my body next to another person can cause her to think I am strange. |
| 2 | I will go to the party because I was invited. I will sit next to the girl in Statistics class because there is an empty seat. | These thoughts are reasonable, so I can keep them. |
| 1 | I am not sure what to say, so I'd better just be quiet. I don't really know that girl, so I won't join her for lunch. | This is probably a good idea. If I am not sure, I can ask for some advice from my support person or a trusted adult. |

## *Ideas and Words to Use When Explaining the Issue of Stalking to a Person With ASD*

- Nonverbal communication such as looks, gestures, etc., is much more important than many people realize. How we look and how we act around other people leads them to have thoughts about who we are and what our intentions are, or what we are thinking about doing. If someone thinks you look mean, they might also think you look dangerous. This may seem unfair, but it is true.

- One way to understand this is to think about our built-in survival instincts. Because our safety requires us to be aware of other people's intentions, we gradually learn to keep track of the people around us. If someone looks or acts in a way that scares us, our natural reaction is to be afraid or at least worried about that person. We can't actually "read" each other's minds, but we can learn to read body language and make some assumptions.

- Some people have difficulty making their face reflect their actual feelings. If you have this problem, you might have good intentions, but your face might look mean. Someone who does not know you well might believe you are mean because your face is sending her that message. If people often think you are mad about something when you are not, you might want to think about studying your facial expressions to see if they are sending the wrong messages.

- Another way nonverbal social communication can be a problem is if you have difficulty reading another person's feelings. This means that you have difficulty guessing how another person feels about you. You might really like someone and want to pursue a relationship with that person, so you ask her out. Maybe she says "no" in a way that is supposed to mean "never," but if you don't "read" the message correctly, you might hear "not today." This could lead you to ask the person out again and again, which could feel odd, strange or even scary to the other person and make her feel uncomfortable about your behavior.

- When someone feels uncomfortable about your behavior, they are likely to seek help. If you work with this person, she might tell the boss that your behavior is scary. If the person thinks you are pursuing her relentlessly, she might call this "stalking." Stalking means to harass or persecute someone with unwanted obsessive attention.
- If someone thinks you are calling too much or showing up at his house uninvited, he might even call the police because stalking is against the law. It is against the law because it is considered threatening behavior, even if you have no plan to hurt the other person.

# Topic: The Words We Use

Having a problem with social cognition appears to impact the ability to notice how one's behavior impacts other people. A common result of poor social cognition includes the use of negative or offensive language without realizing that the words have very troubling consequences. For example, if a young adult is working in a job where he regularly interacts with the public, it is important that he be taught in a very direct way that making comments about a customer's appearance or race could lead to him getting fired.

When we meet a new person who happens to be large, most of us don't even consider telling that person that she is overweight. We realize that a comment like that could be hurtful to the person, and we assume the person already knows that she is large. A very young child might make such blunt comments and be forgiven because of his developmental age. A person on the autism spectrum might be as unaware of another person's feelings about such comments as the young child, but the world is far less forgiving when an adult says offensive things.

The 5-Point Scale can be very useful when either proactively training an employee with ASD or when problem solving a social error that has already happened. If you are charged with supporting a young adult with ASD, it is best not to assume that she automatically knows which topics are and which topics are not well received by customers or co-workers.

By breaking language down into five categories, each representing how words are likely to impact another person, you can more clearly define the social boundaries associated with language. The following is one example, used with a young adult who worked at a fast-food burger shop.

## The Word Scale

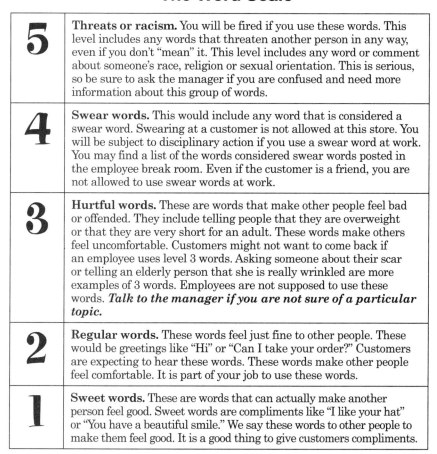

| 5 | **Threats or racism.** You will be fired if you use these words. This level includes any words that threaten another person in any way, even if you don't "mean" it. This level includes any word or comment about someone's race, religion or sexual orientation. This is serious, so be sure to ask the manager if you are confused and need more information about this group of words. |
|---|---|
| 4 | **Swear words.** This would include any word that is considered a swear word. Swearing at a customer is not allowed at this store. You will be subject to disciplinary action if you use a swear word at work. You may find a list of the words considered swear words posted in the employee break room. Even if the customer is a friend, you are not allowed to use swear words at work. |
| 3 | **Hurtful words.** These are words that make other people feel bad or offended. They include telling people that they are overweight or that they are very short for an adult. These words make others feel uncomfortable. Customers might not want to come back if an employee uses level 3 words. Asking someone about their scar or telling an elderly person that she is really wrinkled are more examples of 3 words. Employees are not supposed to use these words. ***Talk to the manager if you are not sure of a particular topic.*** |
| 2 | **Regular words.** These words feel just fine to other people. These would be greetings like "Hi" or "Can I take your order?" Customers are expecting to hear these words. These words make other people feel comfortable. It is part of your job to use these words. |
| 1 | **Sweet words.** These are words that can actually make another person feel good. Sweet words are compliments like "I like your hat" or "You have a beautiful smile." We say these words to other people to make them feel good. It is a good thing to give customers compliments. |

# *Ideas and Words to Use When Explaining the Issue of Offensive Language to a Person With ASD*

- It might sound unreasonable, but words can be just as upsetting as actions when it comes to interacting with other people. You might say something about how a person looks and you might think you are just stating a fact, but what you say might be so offensive to the other person that it could cause you to lose your job, be kicked out of your dorm or lose a friend forever.

- Understanding the "rules of words" is very important for everyone. The words we choose to use can change the way other people think about us in very subtle ways. For example, if you refer to someone as being "fat," anyone who hears you is probably going to think you are rude because the word "fat" is one of those words most people find offensive.

- It is usually not a good idea to state the obvious. If someone has dwarfism, it is not a good idea to point out that she is short. This fact is obvious, and when someone voices it, it sounds like sarcasm. You can safely assume that any comment about someone's physical appearance is risky. Even if you think you are giving the person a compliment, your words might sound rude.

- Swearing is a touchy subject. Some people are almost immune to swearing; they don't seem to even notice when they swear or when someone else swears. This can lead to some big social mistakes. A lot of older people do not like swearing at all. If your boss or your teacher hears you swearing, they might think that you are rude and not very professional. It is important to know when and where it is OK to use swear words.

The best way to keep from making a mistake is to not swear at all. If you want to swear with your friends, make sure there are no other people around who can overhear your conversation. Swearing in a public place is very risky. Most work environments forbid the use of swearing altogether. Finally, it is never a good idea to swear in front of children, elderly folks or people in authority.

# Topic: Creating Friendships

Autism is a social disorder. Individuals on the spectrum will, by definition, have difficulty in social situations. However, contrary to old beliefs, most persons with ASD *do* want to find friends and create relationships. Young adults without friendships are vulnerable to depression, so it is important for support people to pay attention to social isolation even if it looks self-imposed.

There is no "one way" to address friendships or social information, but the 5-Point Scale offers a concrete look at a confusing social dynamic. It is a good idea to support the person's strongest interests and find social connections related to those interests. For example, if the person is an avid chess player, a chess club would be a great place to look for friends.

Think about your own best friends. You probably really care about your friends' interests and talents. You most likely share common interests. A neurotypical individual is more likely to be socially flexible, able to talk about and enjoy the differences in his varied friendships. A person with ASD has fewer and often less flexible social skills, which makes it difficult to easily fit into a variety of social groups. Finding others who can relate to your client or adult child can be the social "leg up" he needs to find the right fit.

Another issue that might be hindering the person's ability to make friends is significantly odd or even "off-putting" behavior, such as reciting lines from favorite movies as a way of contributing to a conversation. Although this might be endearing at a family gathering, it is typically confusing to a group of people who do not know the person well.

This is not to insinuate that a support person should judge the person's love of movies or his talent for remembering the lines. Rather, it is about being honest about how her behavior might be reviewed and interpreted by others. Using a 5-Point Scale is a good way to keep the information factual rather than a reflection of differing opinions.

This scale was used to help a college student realize that his attempts at making friends were actually causing others to reject him. The idea behind the scale was to use a 5 as the worst possible way to meet people and a 1 as a really good way. This scale is highly personalized to this person and his particular behavior.

## A Friendship Scale

| Rating | Ways I Have Tried to Meet Other People and Make Friends | Affirming or Rethinking Your Thoughts |
|---|---|---|
| 5 | I will go to a frat party to find friends. I will drink some beer to be one of the guys. | You are under 21, so drinking is against the law. This is not a good way to meet people. **Rethink:** Stay away from parties where people are drinking. It isn't worth the risk. |
| 4 | I see two people standing together chatting, so I walk up and put my arms around their shoulders so that I am included. | This would be considered strange or even scary behavior. **Rethink:** Approach two people slowly and wait for them to stop talking. Then say "hi." If they do not seem happy to see you, just walk on. |
| 3 | I go to the food court and sit down at a table where other students are eating and say something really funny like, "Nobody expects the Spanish Inquisition." | This will most likely seem very strange to the other students at the table. They likely don't know the context of the quote. **Rethink:** Maybe just walk up to the table. If there is an empty seat, ask if they mind if you join them. |
| 2 | I approach other students in the library or the dorm lounge to see if we have something in common. | This is a pretty good way to meet friends. **Affirmed,** but be sure not to overdo your welcome. If the person does not seem happy to talk with you, just say, "It was nice meeting you" and walk away. |
| 1 | I want to make friends at college, so I look up some activity clubs on campus that interest me. I plan to attend one. | This is a really good idea. **Affirmed!** |

# *Ideas and Words to Use When Explaining the Issue of Finding Friends to a Person With ASD*

- Being social with other people is human. Everyone likes to feel valued and accepted. Finding friends or other people who will like and accept you for who you are is not always easy. Sometimes one person's social behavior doesn't match what other people are expecting. When this happens, you might accidentally scare others. Problems with making friends does not mean that there is something wrong with you or that what you are doing is bad. It just means that what you are doing looks or feels really different to the other people. When this happens, they may not be open to being your friend.
- There are two especially good ways to find friends. The first is to seek out people who love the same things you love. If you have an interest in astronomy, the best place to start is by taking a class in astronomy or looking for an astronomy club in your community. If you are really interested in animals, take a class in the animal science department or volunteer at the Humane Society or Animal Rescue. The idea is to find other people who want to talk about the same things you want to talk about and do the same things you want to do.
- The second thing you can do is use the 5-Point Scale to evaluate the friendship-making efforts you have made. If you haven't had much success, maybe it's because your behavior seemed too abrupt or different, leaving the other person confused about your intentions. For example, maybe you want to be friends, but your tone of voice sounds insulting. It might be a good idea to ask a good friend, parent or counselor to help you with this because they can give you a second opinion. For example, you might think the people who rejected you were mean, but a trusted person might be able to see your behavior from a different perspective, explain how others may interpret your behavior and help you come up with some new and better friendship-making ideas.

# Topic: Dating

Relationships in general are difficult for people with ASD, and strong emotional relationships are even more difficult. Many adults with ASD talk about wanting a boyfriend or a girlfriend and about getting married some day. It is important to talk about relationships in a very concrete and direct way so that the person on the spectrum can learn the cognitive skills needed to begin and continue meaningful relationships.

When the person you support expresses frustration about not having a girlfriend or a boyfriend, it is not helpful to say things like, "It will happen some day." Statements like this do not teach the skills this person is likely lacking. Most of us can agree that forming and maintaining a serious relationship is one of life's most difficult endeavors. At the very least, a person on the spectrum will need some support in this area.

It is a good idea to break down the facts about dating and forming emotional relationships in the same way we do when teaching other skills. For example, teaching the difference between a stranger, an acquaintance and a friend is important for making decisions about social boundaries. If the person you support invites strangers to his room, this could put him in a vulnerable and possibly dangerous position.

Teaching somebody to recognize the difference between a friend and a boyfriend or a girlfriend is not easy. This skill involves recognizing emotions in oneself, reading the emotions of others and knowing when the two sets of emotions are communicating mutual desire. If the person you support misreads another person's emotions, she is likely to make social-boundary mistakes that could be very hurtful, embarrassing or even dangerous.

Being rejected is hard for anyone, and the person with ASD is likely to be hurt and terribly confused by what he is doing wrong. Anxiety and frustration can build in these situations, so it is important to take the time to not only teach needed skills but also to help the person understand what strategies might not be effective. Compassionate honesty is often needed in these situations.

The following are examples of two scales that were used to help a person better understand dating and relationships. These scales are only examples. It is important to individualize the information on a scale so that the person you are supporting can directly relate to the information and the proposed solutions.

## A Scale for Defining Relationships

| Rating | A Word for This | Define This Level |
|---|---|---|
| 5 | Intimate relationship/ spouse | This is someone you share your life with and trust completely. This person is your life partner; he/she supports you and you support him/her. There is usually physical intimacy involved. |
| 4 | Boyfriend/girlfriend | This is someone you want to be with a lot. You are a couple, and you usually make future plans together. There is usually kissing or other intimate touching involved. |
| 3 | Friend | This is someone you know and trust. Somebody who enjoys things that you enjoy, who likes you and who you like spending time with. You might go to this person's house. |
| 2 | Acquaintance | This is someone you have met informally, like at work or in class. You might see the person every day, but you don't really know very much about him/her. This might also be someone who never really became a friend even though you have known, him/her a long time. |
| 1 | Stranger | This is someone you have just met. You do not know this person yet. Get to know this person in a public or social setting. |

# A Scale for Working Through Dating Decisions

*If you meet someone and you are interested in getting to know that person better, you might want to think about what level of this scale you are at and what level your "someone" is at. There are many different kinds of friendships. You might feel like a 5 and your "someone" might only feel like a 3. If you are unsure about how the other person feels, it is a good idea to start with 2 or 3.*

| Rating | What Are Your Thoughts and Feelings About This Relationship? |
|---|---|
| **5** | I really like this person and would like to date him/her exclusively. |
| **4** | I like this person and would like to go on a date and see what happens. I would like to exchange phone numbers. |
| **3** | I am interested in e-mailing this person from time to time and see if it develops into dating. I don't want to exchange phone numbers yet. |
| **2** | I am interested in being friends with this person, but I am not interested in dating. I would be OK with exchanging e-mail addresses, but I don't think the relationship will lead to dating. |
| **1** | I am not interested in a relationship with this person at all. Let's just say goodbye and leave it at that. |

# Some Ideas and Words to Use When Explaining Dating to a Person With ASD

- Dating is difficult for everyone. Some people make it look easy, but most people agree that it is not. For example, we sometimes see couples that look very comfortable with each other. They have probably known each other for a long time, or maybe they share a lot of interests. Guessing how someone else feels emotionally is part of dating, and this is never easy.

Such guessing involves "reading" nonverbal language such as facial expressions, tone of voice, personal social distance, and figuring out how the other person feels.

- People you do not know well are considered strangers. If you have met someone once, he or she might still consider you a stranger. Since we don't usually ask strangers out on a date, you should get to know the person a bit more before considering asking for a date.

- Once you start to get to know someone (by talking at work or a party, sitting near each other in class or working in a group together), they can be considered an acquaintance. This is an acceptable time to ask someone out on a date. But everyone has different comfort levels about this, so don't be offended if the person is not ready for the closeness of a 1:1 date.

- When you have spent a lot of time with someone in different social situations, you are likely to be in a better position to feel that there is a certain level of respect and trust between the two of you. If you start to have romantic feelings about someone like this, you can probably ask for a date and expect an honest answer. The answer might be "no," but that does not mean the person doesn't want to remain friends. It usually means that his or her feelings are not at the same level as yours.

Remember that once you begin to date, some people take a really long time to feel strong emotions for another person, but others fall in love in 20 minutes! This makes relationships very tricky, especially in the beginning. If you find that you are always "misreading" other people's feelings, a scale might be helpful for you.

- If you find dating very hard, try talking to people you know who are in a romantic relationship. Ask them how they met and what kinds of things they like to do together. A trusted adult can also help you work through some of the dating questions, like how to move from just being friends to a dating relationship.

# Topic: Dealing With Roommates

When an individual with ASD moves out of the house, there is a temptation for parents and other caregivers to assume that everything else will just fall in place for the person. You might be hopeful that the person you support will find a friend, become best friends with a roommate and be included in the social networks that typically evolve around apartment or dorm life. However, if the person with ASD had difficulty with social situations in the past, it is important to address the social pressures of living on campus or in a community environment prior to moving into a roommate situation.

If you think back to your own early experiences with roommates, you may recall how difficult it can be to navigate the minefield that a forced communal living situation can be for any of us. Without some guidance, training or even direct intervention, adults on the autism spectrum may miss out on the seemingly easy and natural development of social connections that other young adults enjoy. In addition, if the first attempt to find a compatible roommate does not work out, it can be a blow to the person's confidence and negatively impact her willingness to try again.

The most common mistakes individuals with ASD make when entering a new living situation are related to their natural black-and-white thinking. Some treat a roommate as a best friend with an uncomfortable level of familiarity, others ignore their roommates to a degree that feels odd or uncomfortable.

If the person with ASD feels that roommate status automatically means best friend status, he might take liberties with the roommate's food, clothing or other possessions, or he might assume that if the roommate is invited to a party, he is automatically invited as well.

On the other hand, a person with ASD might translate sharing a room as very literally "sharing" space and nothing more. She might act as if her roommate is invisible, never speaking to her, or even divide the room down the middle to set rigid boundaries.

Scales can be used to clarify each roommate's thoughts about topics of co-habitation or as a system for discussing black-and-white thinking as it relates to the "gray" areas of living with another person. The following are two examples of how scales have been used to clarify and problem-solve social interactions. The first scale is an activity that a support person can do with the new roommate(s) to help everyone understand the nature of living with a person who did not grow up in their own family. Each person's perspective and tolerance level is rated, giving roommates insight into how they each think about these varied topics.

The second scale is an example of a scale that was used to clarify how a particular individual on the spectrum was processing or thinking through social decisions regarding her roommate. This is only an example, and the issues will be different for different people. Using the format of "these are my first thoughts" and "this is how I might rethink the situation," a support person can concretely explain the social errors in the person's thinking.

## Common Roommate Issues

- Roommate eats my food.
- Roommate labels everything and does not share anything.
- Roommate leaves underwear on the floor of the living room.
- Roommate does not do dishes.
- Roommate gets a pet.
- Roommate brings friends home during the week.

- Roommate brings friends home and lets them stay all night.
- Roommate never cleans his room.
- Roommate does not help clean the common living spaces.
- Roommate does not wash his clothes; he stinks.
- Roommate does not pay rent on time.
- Roommate smokes.
- Roommate does not try to conserve energy.
- Roommate collects too much stuff like a hoarder.
- Roommate comes in late and is really loud.
- Roommate borrows my clothes without asking.
- Roommate uses my toiletries.
- Roommate's friend goes into my room.

## Scale to Rate Common Roommate Issues

| Rating | This Is How It Might Make Me Feel and Think | This is What Would Probably Happen |
|---|---|---|
| 5 | This is a deal breaker. | I would move out. Please never do this! |
| 4 | This is very upsetting. Maybe I should find a new roommate. | I would ask for a serious meeting. |
| 3 | This would irritate me, and I would have to say something to my roommate about it. | I might be able to compromise, but we would need to talk about it. |
| 2 | This would bother me. | I might not say anything, but it would bug me. |
| 1 | This wouldn't bother me at all. I am very comfortable with this. | Nothing. |

## Scale to Guide a Conversation About Social Thinking

| Rating | These Are My First Thoughts | This Is How I Might Rethink the Situation |
|---|---|---|
| 5 | Since we live in the same room, I will eat my roommate's food when I am out of snacks. I can borrow her clothes when mine are dirty. | This could be a violation of the college's conduct code. I may be kicked out of the dorm for this behavior. |
| 4 | On my Facebook page, I write that my roommate and I live together and go to school together. | Talking about someone without their permission on Facebook can be considered a privacy violation. This is not OK. |
| 3 | My roommate is going home this weekend. I will pack and be ready to go with her. | If my roommate has not specifically invited me to go with her, then I am not invited. I could ask her if she would like me to water her plants or pick up her mail while she is gone. |
| 2 | We are roommates, so I will eat meals when my roommate does so that we are on the same schedule. I will follow her to the dining hall for every meal. | Following the same schedule as my roommate is not necessary. I should ask my roommate if I can join her for meals when we are both back at the dorm at the same time. |
| 1 | My roommate and I are sharing space. It would be nice to be friends too, but this might not happen. | I can try to be polite and respectful of differences. I can ask my residential life advisor for some tips on getting to know my roommate better. |

## Ideas and Words to Use When Explaining Living With Roommates to a Person With ASD

- Living with a roommate can be harder than you think. Most of us have lived our entire lives with one family, and every family has its own routines and unspoken rules to live by. When you move out of your family home and into a dorm room, apartment or house with a roommate, it might be hard at first to navigate the new relationship. Your roommate's family had its own routines and unspoken rules too, and they might not be the same as yours.
- In many instances, this roommate is a stranger. For example, if you are going to college and planning to live in the dorm, you might be randomly assigned a room and a roommate. Even if you know the person and have picked the person to be your roommate, living together is a bit more difficult than just being that person's friend.
- It can be helpful to think about how you and the other members of your family compromise. If you have brothers or sisters, you know that sometimes one person wants to watch one TV show and another wants to watch a different show. If you only had one TV, how would your family work it out?
- Roommates share space, but roommates are not always friends. Friendships have to be nurtured, and they might take a long time to develop. Some roommates never become really good friends, but they learn to share space effectively and respect each other's differences.
- It is not unusual to have high expectations for your first roommate. You might want this person to be your best friend and to do everything together. Try not to be disappointed if your roommate chooses to hang out with other

people. It is great when roommates become friends, but it doesn't always happen.

- Sharing space means that your roommate's food and clothing will be in the same space as well. It is a good idea to talk openly about how comfortable you and your roommate are about sharing things. If someone buys a jar of peanut butter and assumes he is the only one eating it, he might plan for it to last a month. It would be upsetting for this person to realize that someone else is eating it, too. On the other hand, maybe your roommate wants to share and you do, too. Then a conversation about how that sharing might look is a good idea.

- Cleaning up after yourself and living with someone who cleans up after himself is another big deal with roommates. If you or your roommate feels that the other is not helping to keep the room or apartment clean, there are likely to be problems. Some roommates post a schedule of cleaning that needs to be done and maybe even a note about whose turn it is to do what. If you are in a dorm room, it might just involve keeping your clothes picked up and your belongings on your side of the room. If you are in an apartment, it could involve washing dishes, wiping counters, sweeping and vacuuming.

- Respect for your roommate's privacy is very important. Bringing other people to your room or apartment might feel uncomfortable to your roommate. Be sure to discuss this with your roommate since everybody has different privacy needs. Using a rating scale to review some common roommate issues might help you to understand your roommate's perspective and plan for your differences.

# Topic: Issues in the Workplace

Autism involves problems with social thinking which, by definition, means that a person might have the highly developed technical skills needed to do a certain job but lack the common sense or judgment skills needed to successfully work with other people.

It is highly recommended that people with ASD get some experience with employment as early as possible. If the person is living at home, the job might be very informal, such as dog walking for neighbors or delivering papers. One objective of early employment is to give the person experiences that require attending to and listening to a "boss" who is not a family member.

The fact that the boss is the boss and that arguing with or insulting the boss can lead to being fired might seem unreasonable or unfair to a person on the spectrum. After such an unfortunate situation has occurred, it is important to address any significant social mistakes the person with ASD made that led to the firing. Even when the reasons for conflict seem obvious to others, the person on the spectrum might not fully understand, and this impacts his ability to learn from his mistakes.

Following are two scales that were used to problem-solve in the workplace. The first scale was developed for a young man who had been fired from several jobs for insubordination and social misconduct. The scale was used to help him organize errors in his thinking. The support person systematically outlined his erroneous thinking in one column and suggested a new way to think about the situation in the other.

The second scale is more simplistic, used with a young man who was complaining about his job. His supervisor talked to him about the situation, but the young man continued to voice his complaints and did not seem to understand that it could lead to being fired since, in his words, "He knew of other people who had been fired and their behavior had been much worse than his." The scale helped him to understand that there are different "levels" of problems at work, and it is not just the "worst" behavior that can get you fired.

## Workplace Issues Scale #1

| Rating | These Are My First Thoughts | This Is How I Might Rethink the Situation |
|---|---|---|
| 5 | I don't like what my boss tells me to do! I know more about this job than he does. I will tell him what I think of him. | This is called insubordination, even if you think you are right. In most cases, *you will be fired* for this kind of behavior. |
| 4 | I think my supervisor is pretty, so I will tell her she has a good body. | This comment is most likely upsetting to any supervisor. It shows poor judgment and **you might get fired** for saying it. Remember that you don't need to say everything you think. |
| 3 | When I take a break in the staff lounge, I lie down and take a nap because it's called a "lounge." | You should never sleep on your job unless you have special permission from the boss. A staff lounge is usually intended to be used for short breaks. |
| 2 | I will work slowly or pretend I am busy so my supervisor won't assign me more work. | This could look like laziness to your boss and coworkers. It might not get you fired, but it won't make you any friends. |
| 1 | I have finished my work and am not sure what to do next. I will ask my supervisor for some guidance on what tasks he needs me to do. | This is probably a good idea. |

## Workplace Issues Scale #2

| Rating | What I Did | Likely Outcome |
|--------|-----------|----------------|
| **5** | Swearing at a customer. Fighting or frightening a coworker. | *You will be fired.* |
| **4** | Taking materials home from work without permission. | This could be viewed as stealing, and **you could be fired for it.** |
| **3** | Complaining about the job to others at work. | Your supervisor will talk to you about the proper way to voice a complaint. **You might be fired if it continues.** |
| **2** | Being late; working slowly; leaving early; taking long lunches. | Your coworkers will notice this. They might think it is unfair since everyone else was on time. Coworkers might complain to your boss. |
| **1** | Being on time; smiling at customers; using a pleasant voice tone; following posted protocols. | These are all expected behaviors for the job. You are most likely acting in a way that pleases your boss. You should get a good evaluation. |

# *Ideas and Words to Use When Explaining Workplace Issues to a Person With ASD*

- Having a job is an important part of being an adult. When you are no longer in school, a job is what you do all day and how you make money. When you are still in school, you might have a part-time job to help pay for basic supplies or just to have spending money. Getting some early experiences in a job will help you handle the day-to-day problems that can arise in a work setting.
- Every job has value. You might be working a job just to earn some spending money, but you can still get fired if you don't understand and follow the rules. Most bosses

want workers to get along, and you will likely get fired if you are rude to either your coworkers or the customers. It is important to understand what behaviors are considered rude because what seems reasonable to you might be so upsetting to your boss that you lose your job.

- Depending on what type of job you get, you will be expected to complete a certain amount of work. You can ask your supervisor to clearly explain his expectations for you each day. Be sure to ask about dress code and other rules of social conduct in your particular work place.

- If you are having difficulty understanding the importance of responsible behavior on the job, try working it through with a supportive adult and a 5-Point Scale. Sometimes it is also a good idea to include your supervisor in this discussion to be sure the information on your scale is true and accurate.

# Part Two:
# Creating Scales in the Moment

We hope that you have gained a clear understanding of the ideas that support the use of the 5-Point Scale. The scale is a systematic approach to teaching social concepts and information needed for successful emotional regulation. For example, it can take a very sensitive issue and put it into a nonpersonal context, making it easier to address. The 5-Point Scale is not meant to be a behavior management tool but a self-management or self-realization tool. Nowhere is this type of support more crucial than for adults because breaches in social rules at this point in life can lead to life-long consequences, including losing a job, losing a housing opportunity, and even ending up in jail.

In Part One, we listed some common areas of social mis-understanding or emotional dysregulation and illustrated with corresponding scales. The next level of understanding how to flexibly use a scale involves using the method in real and spontaneous situations. Social behavior doesn't happen in a vacuum, and we can't predict what challenges are on the horizon.

In the following, we present some examples of how a 5-Point Scale was used "in the moment" to support a person who desperately needed some honest information. (Sometimes the scales are just written on a piece of scrap paper or a napkin.) The idea is to use the system to visually process a difficult situation.

# Topic: Behavior Towards Other People

*This scale was used with a young man who asked provocative questions of his coworkers. He was in jeopardy of being fired if he did not stop this behavior. The scale was used successfully to help him understand how his words made other people think about him.*

| Rating | A Good Word for It | People Might Think This About You | Examples of This Level |
|---|---|---|---|
| 5 | Threatening | He is dangerous. I should call the police or report him to the boss. | Bringing a weapon to work. Telling people that you want to kill them. |
| 4 | Scary | I don't want to work near this person. He seems scary. | Asking people if they would be afraid if you brought a gun to work. |
| 3 | Strange | I can't figure this person out. I don't know how to think about him. | Repeating lines from movies. Grabbing someone's arm unexpectedly. |
| 2 | OK | OK. I might want to be his friend. | Saying "Good morning." Smiling at people when they smile at you. |
| 1 | Great | I really like this guy. I want to work next to him. I feel happy when he is at work. | Giving compliments. Sharing materials. Offering to help someone. |

# Topic: Classroom Outbursts

*This scale was developed to help a student who had exhibited explosive behavior in the classroom. He had lost control, and was told that if he ever had an outburst in class again, he would be dropped from the course. The goal of the scale was to help the student understand the different levels of "being in class" in hopes of helping him to understand his state of mind and, therefore, remain in control and make better decisions.*

| Rating | What Does This Level Look Like? |
|---|---|
| 5 | Outburst; throwing things; yelling out in class. **This is not allowed in college classes. You will not be allowed to return to the course.** |
| 4 | Nervous or upset; interrupting the professor; clenching hands and trying not to speak out. This is a good time to leave class. You will be allowed to continue in the class if you can leave before you get to a 5. |
| 3 | Listening in class; taking notes; participating when called on. **This is expected behavior in college.** |
| 2 | Attending class but not paying attention; allowing your mind to drift; not taking notes. This is not an effective way to attend class. Your notes and grade will probably suffer. |
| 1 | Deciding to skip class. You will miss the information. This could lead to failing the class. |

# Topic: Dorm Behavior

*This scale was developed to help a college student who had trouble remembering to put on a towel or a bathrobe when he left his dorm room to go to the bathroom down the hall. He did not seem to intuitively understand that walking around naked made the other students on his dorm floor uncomfortable.*

| Rating | What? | Likely Outcome |
|---|---|---|
| **5** | Walking naked in the hallway for any reason. | You will be asked to move out of the dorm. |
| **4** | Holding a towel in front of yourself and running for the bathroom. | Not OK. This is offensive and could look upsetting to other students. Someone is likely to report you to residential life staff. |
| **3** | Wrapping a towel around your waist and tucking it into one side securely. | This is risky because towels are not always secure. The towel could fall open, leaving you exposed, and upset someone. It is an option if you have no other choices. |
| **2** | Wearing a large robe in the hallway on the way to the bathroom. The robe should cover your private body areas completely. | This is good and practical. Remember that the robe should only be used to walk to and from the bathroom or in your room. It is not OK to wear the robe in the TV lounge or down to the cafeteria. |
| **1** | Walking to the bathroom or in the hallway fully dressed. | This is the safest choice. This is considerate of other people's space and feelings. |

# Topic: Is It an Emergency?

*This scale was used to discuss emergency situations to a young man who repeatedly called 911 when he was feeling confused. His support people had told him that it was against the law to call 911 unless it was a true emergency, but he was not able to distinguish between feeling confused or even a little scared and a true emergency.*

| Rating | What Might This Look Like? | What Should You Do? |
|---|---|---|
| 5 | You are robbed, assaulted or physically hurt. | Call 911. |
| 4 | You are stopped or questioned by the police or another authorized person or even arrested. | Do not run away. Carry emergency phone numbers of your support people and ask to call. Consider carrying a prepared statement that explains that you have an autism spectrum disorder. |
| 3 | You see a dangerous situation like a fire, or you witness a crime. | Get to a safe place and call 911 to report the situation. |
| 2 | You run out of money and are not able to pay for something. | Tell the cashier that you need to leave and get money. If in a restaurant, call a support person or trusted friend for help. Don't run out of a restaurant without paying. |
| 1 | You are in a confusing situation like getting off at the wrong bus stop or going to the store and finding it closed. | Call someone you trust. Carry a map when you travel. Ask a police officer or someone in an official uniform for assistance. |

# Topic: Group Work

*This scale was developed for a young woman who was refusing to work in groups in a college class that required many group projects. She experienced a high level of stress associated with compromise and could be very critical of others' ideas or comments. The instructor had told the student's support person that she would be dropped from the class unless she completed group work.*

| Rating | What Are You Thinking? What Is Your Self-talk? | What Is the Likely Outcome of This Kind of Thinking? |
|---|---|---|
| **5** | I am not going to work with other people! | You will be asked to withdraw from the class. |
| **4** | I will work in the stupid group but will insist on things being done my way. I know best! | This is not good thinking. Group work is all about compromise. You might get a bad grade even though you participated. |
| **3** | I will work with the group but will tell everyone what I think of their ideas if I don't like them. I will not hold back on my honesty. | This thinking will probably get you into trouble. There is a time and place for honesty, but when you work in a group, you need to hold off on cold, objective assessment of others' ideas. |
| **2** | I will work with the group for a short period of time and take lots of breaks to relax. | This might be OK with your instructor, and it is a way to build tolerance. This shows a willingness to try even though it is hard for you. |
| **1** | I will work with my assigned group even though it is hard for me. I will try to say something nice about someone else's idea even if I don't like it. | **This is the ultimate goal.** It is not always easy to work in groups, but it is a required skill in some classes and in many jobs. |

# Topic: Handling Obsessive Behavior

*This scale was used with a young adult who had frequent bouts of anxiety that would cause him to blow his nose. His repetitive nose blowing was upsetting to his coworkers and led them to complain to the boss. The focus of his plan was on relaxation, and he reviewed the scale each morning before work.*

| Rating | This Is What It Feels Like | This Is What I Can Try to Do |
|---|---|---|
| **5** | I am blowing my nose constantly. I feel like my head is going to explode. I have no energy to think about other people. | I need to ask my boss if I can work in an isolated area today. I might have to go home. I should meet with my support person and discuss my relaxation program. |
| **4** | I am blowing my nose a lot this morning. I have a tingling sensation in my whole body. People are looking at me a lot. | This is when my OCD is beginning to take over my brain. I need some more extensive relaxation this morning before starting my work. |
| **3** | My brain is running a little fast today. My body is starting to tingle and my nose is running. | I will start my day with 5 minutes of relaxation exercise from my plan. I will be sure to wash my hands if I need to blow my nose a lot. |
| **2** | My nose has been a little runny this morning. | I will make a mental note that this is happening. I will make sure I have a clean handkerchief or tissue in my pocket. |
| **1** | I am comfortable. My body and head feel calm and quiet. | I will enjoy the moment and, hopefully, the day. ☺ |

# Conclusion

By Jane Thierfeld Brown and Lisa King

**W**e have been working with young adults with disabilities for a combined 50 years. Navigating the dating world or understanding the tricky nature of the workplace or life on a college campus can be difficult for even the most skillful young adults. Most of us have memories from our early 20s of behaviors we regret and social situations we lament. Yet, most of us went through this time with well-developed social cognition skills.

It has only been in recent years that those of us serving in the adult support capacity have begun rethinking challenging behavior as it relates to social cognition. This new approach to addressing behavior involves direct teaching of social cognitive skills, regardless of the person's age. One of our very favorite approaches is the use of a 5-Point Scale, originally presented by Buron and Curtis in their landmark book, *The Incredible 5-Point Scale.* We have used it with many young adults (on campus, in the community and in the work place) to assist them in integrating into society. Many young people with ASD have told us that understanding and using these scales helped them in multiple environments.

After using the method successfully for a number of years, we decided to explore the idea of a 5-Point Scale book focused on adult issues and addressed to adult service providers. Understanding adolescent and adult behavior is challenging. In this book we have attempted to explain how to use the scale as a system to explain, and work through, some difficult behavioral and emotional concepts. The challenges discussed severely impact the social success of a person with ASD. Our hope is that the scale approach will increase understanding for individuals on the spectrum and their supporters.

In our work at colleges (Wolf, Thierfeld Brown, & Bork, 2009), we found the 5-Point Scale useful, not only to students but also to the people on campus who worked with them – counselors, disability services, residence life staff and professors. We trained professionals to help students develop scales for understanding behavior and for controlling stress and anxiety. The students told us that this worked for them and that by making small, business card-sized scales they could carry the scale with them as reminders during the day or if in crisis.

One student developed a scale to remind himself to be calm while walking to class so that his anxiety wouldn't overwhelm him, making it difficult for him to stay in the class.

This student needed to remind himself of how the anxiety manifested in physical symptoms.

| | |
|---|---|
| **5** | Losing control. Overwhelmed. **Avoid going into the classroom at this level.** |
| **4** | Clenching fists. Getting wound up. **Take deep breaths.** |
| **3** | Looking around. Thinking about too many things. Talking out loud to myself. This means I am getting overstimulated. **Try to focus on walking slowly.** |
| **2** | Some anxiety, walking fast, taking short breaths. **Slow down a bit.** |
| **1** | Walking to class with a relaxed body. Feels soft. **Keep it up!** |

If the student was feeling too stressed (at a 3 or higher), he would go through the scale backward, gradually pulling himself down to a 1 or a 2. He was then able to walk into the lecture hall and remain there through the class.

Our goal in this volume is to demonstrate the versatility of the scales by illustrating examples as they relate to issues commonly faced by young adults on the autism spectrum. Our hope is that we have given you enough ideas to grasp the concept connected to the scale, relate it to the adult population and adult experiences and to adapt it to the specific needs of persons you support.

# References

Attwood, T. (2006). *The complete guide to Asperger's syndrome.* London, UK: Jessica Kingsley Publishing.

Buron, K. D., & Curtis, M. B. (2012). *The incredible 5-point scale – The significantly improved second edition: Assisting students with autism spectrum disorders in understanding social interactions and controlling their emotional responses.* Shawnee Mission, KS: AAPC Publishing.

Golan, O., & Baron-Cohen, S. (2009). Systemizing emotions: Teaching people on the autism spectrum to recognize emotions using interactive multimedia. In K. D. Buron & P. Wolfberg (Eds.), *Learners on the autism spectrum: Preparing highly qualified educators* (pp. 234-253). Shawnee Mission, KS: AAPC Publishing.

Wolf, L., Thierfeld Brown, J., & Bork, R. (2009). *Students with Asperger Syndrome: A guide for college personnel.* Shawnee Mission, KS: AAPC Publishing.

## About the Authors:

**Kari Dunn Buron, MS,** taught students on the autism spectrum for more than 30 years in K-12. She developed an autism spectrum disorders certificate program for educators at Hamline University in St. Paul, Minnesota, and has done volunteer work specific to autism in Trinidad, Tobago, Barbados, Tanzania and Ghana. Kari is the co-author of *The Incredible 5-Point Scale* and the author of *When My Worries Get Too Big, A 5 Could Make Me Lose Control* and *A 5 is Against the Law!* (2008 ASA Literary Award Winner). She is also the co-editor of a textbook for educators entitled *Learners on the Autism Spectrum: Preparing Highly Qualified Educators* (2009 ASA Literary Award Winner) and the creator of *The Social Times,* a social skills magazine (2010 Gold Winner, National Parenting Publications Award, and Gold Medal Winner, Moonbeam Children's Book Awards).

**Jane Thierfeld Brown, EdD,** is director of student services at the University of Connecticut School of Law. She has worked in disability services for 33 years. Jane's main research interests are students with autism spectrum disorders in higher education and students with disabilities in high-stakes graduate programs. She consults with many institutions of higher education, as well as with parents and students on issues of students with autism spectrum disorders, and is a frequent keynote speaker at conferences. She co-authored *Students With Asperger Syndrome: A Guide for College Personnel* and *The Parent's Guide to College for Students on the Autism Spectrum.* Jane has three children, the youngest of whom is a 20-year-old son on the spectrum.

**Mitzi Beth Curtis, MsEd,** is an autism resource specialist currently working for Intermediate School District 287 in Minnesota, and consulting with Minnesota Life College. She has worked in special education, supported employment and residential programs for individuals with disabilities since 1978. Mitzi's youngest sister, Maria, sent her on this journey with her birth in 1963.

**Lisa King, MEd,** is a co-director of College Autism Spectrum, an educational consulting company that provides training and guidance to colleges regarding best practices for working with students on the autism spectrum, in addition to working directly with students on the spectrum and their families as they transition to, through and beyond college. Additionally, she serves as an access consultant for St. Catherine University. Lisa led a two-year pilot program at the University of Minnesota, implementing a new model of service: Strategic Education for Asperger Students. She co-authored *The Parent's Guide to College for Students on the Autism Spectrum.* Lisa is a wife to Chris and mother of Ian and Bryn.

P.O. Box 23173
Shawnee Mission, Kansas 66283-0173
www.aapcpublishing.net